Daughters, Guns, and Bibles:
Raising Godly Daughters in an Ungodly World

By: Carolyn Gullett

Copyright © 2012 by Carolyn Gullett

Daughters, Guns, and Bibles
by Carolyn Gullett

Printed in the United States of America

ISBN 9781622300075

All rights reserved solely by the author. The author guarantees all contents are original and do not infringe upon the legal rights of any other person or work. No part of this book may be reproduced in any form without the permission of the author. The views expressed in this book are not necessarily those of the publisher.

Unless otherwise indicated, Bible quotations are taken from the New King James Version. Copyright © 1982 by Thomas Nelson Bibles.

www.xulonpress.com

Acknowledgments

I give thanks to my loving heavenly Father for whom I'm grateful for the grace given to me to write this book. If it had not been for His voice telling me to write this book, it would not have been done.

I give thanks to my gorgeous husband, Delmar who encouraged me faithfully to keep writing.

I give thanks to all my church family who encouraged me along the way and gave of their precious time to answer questions and give feedback.

A special thank you to Marc Stefanski, CEO/President/Chairman of Third Federal S & L. Because of the stock he gave to his associates in February 2010 for Valentine's Day, that stock was used to help finance the publishing of this book.

Table of Contents

Preface ix
Introduction xi
Daughters 13
Heaven on Earth 15
Values Over Good Looks. 22
Communication 26
Actions Speak Louder Than Words. 30
Love in Action 34
Unequally Yoked 44
Is He the Right One?. 53
Father Knows Best 57
Deception 60
So Your Daughter Wants To Date 65
Hope 69
Questions and Answers. 75

Preface

*I*t was May 11, 2009 in Fort Myers, Florida. I was driving home from work on Hwy 82. I had been rehearsing in my head what to tell a young lady regarding the reasons she should not marry this guy. I said to myself, "That is good, I should write a book and call it: The Daughter, The Gun and the Bible.

Immediately I dismissed that thought. I had no intentions on writing a book. That was like asking me to run for the presidency. That was on a Monday. On Tuesday morning, I made my way to Morning Prayer at the church. As I paced the floor in the back of the sanctuary praying, I heard a voice that seemed to come from above me say these words; write the book. Stunned, I looked upward to see where the voice came from and then behind me but, no one was there. I was puzzled to say the least and forgot about it until Wednesday night service. Standing on the front row minding my own business and listening to my pastor exhort, the first line of the book dropped in my spirit. I knew immediately that it was the Holy Spirit. So I said to myself, I guess I am writing a book. With excitement, I sat and penned the first line of the book. I can't tell you how excited I was. Thursday morning during my time of prayer, I decided to write down the first line of the book. To my amazement the Holy Spirit gave me a whole page to write. The rest is history. All glory to God!

Introduction

*D*aughters have a special place in our hearts- even more special I think for fathers. If he has a son it denotes somehow his manhood and his chest seems to swell, like Tarzan and he roars. It also means that his last name is carried on. A daughter seems to melt a father and you may see a side of him you didn't know existed. Daughters are more precious and we see them as delicate flowers. Beware to the young man who sets his eye on her. He may be surprised to find out what could happen to him by pursuing our precious flower called," my daughter.

Daughters

Have you ever wondered why daughters bring home a young man and expect you to accept him without any questions? Her eyes are beaming and she has a smile from one ear to the other. Her heart perhaps racing and thinking I hope my parent(s) like him. Of course, she thinks he is wonderful and there's nothing wrong with him. On the other hand she's probably hoping dad won't embarrass her.

Usually the mom is excited for her little girl and anxious to meet the young man. The dad may have already cleaned and loaded his gun in hopes of running the poor guy off. Nevertheless, this day is inevitable. I'm sure many of you are recanting what happened to you when you invited your boyfriend or girlfriend over to meet the parents. That's probably another book in itself.

Daughters, Guns, and Bibles

If you are parents of a daughter, think back to the day she was born. You held her in your arms with great joy. Adoring everything about her you began counting her toes and fingers. You began noticing the color of her hair. Hopefully she did have hair. You would point out whose nose she had and the color of her eyes. You would pronounce her perfect. The moment that baby girl smiled, dad was done for. From that day on she would probably have dad wrapped around her finger. If dad did not have a gun when she was born he was on his way to purchase one and may even take shooting lessons.

I know that this is not always the case, but I wouldn't be surprised if it happened. His new mission in life now is to protect his daughter from the so called boyfriend. After all, he was a young man at one time. Some fathers don't plan on their little girl leaving home. He has been her provider, protector and father and wants to keep her safe in the castle. Young men may be viewed as the dragon so to speak. Dad wants to protect his daughter from the possible heartbreaks that go along with dating. He may feel that no young man is good enough for her.

Heaven on Earth

Generations have shown us that some girls tend to select men that remind them of their father. This choice can be good or bad. There is a great responsibility on the father to nurture his daughter according to Gods plan. She needs a role model to go by. This can be done in the home as she observes how mom and dad relate to one another. This is crucial and forms the basis for which the daughter would want to model her relationship with her husband. The home environment should be the happiest place for us. Deuteronomy 11:21 reads," that your days and the days of your children may be multiplied in the land of which the Lord swore to your fathers to give them, like the days of the heavens on earth."

Imagine that. God our heavenly Father desires that

we experience heaven on earth in our relationships. Can you imagine a home filled with laughter, joy, peace and love? A home where everyone is encouraged, uplifted and valued. Wow, is that possible? It most certainly is. I believe that whatever God has purposed for mankind is possible if we follow His instructions. In order to do that, we must have a relationship with God. He desires to communicate with us. The book of Proverbs says that wisdom was His companion and by understanding He created the heavens and the earth. We can trust His instruction in our relationships.

If you can recall your childhood, you probably experienced some things you wished never happened or some things you wished could last forever. Some of us may have or are raising our children in the manner we were raised. We are products of what our parents instilled in us. Our behaviors, beliefs and morals stem from our childhood. There are times we do and say the same things our parents did. We may have said as a child we would not repeat the behavior of our parents. I recall my husband telling me early in our marriage that as a teenager he made a conscious decision that he would not repeat the negative behavior of his family. And I'm happy to say that he has done well.

Some of us grew up hearing our parents yell at each other, yell at us, throw things, slam doors, drink themselves silly and curse to no end. And some have had the misfortune of abuse, verbal and physical. Sometimes the parent would even take out their frustrations on you the child. This is just a few of the things that make for a bad example for our children. This is not experiencing heaven on earth. As history repeats itself from generation to generation, how can we stop this? The answer is the word of God. But we need to be diligent in applying the word. It's not enough to know, we must be doers. When men take a stand and commit to being the leader in the home under Gods direction, they will raise boys to be men of God for our daughters and they become mighty in the earth.

Unfortunately some of us have left a dysfunctional home and started one of our own. How sad this must make our creator, who said, let us make man in our image. The bible has something to say regarding the function of the home and how parents are to treat one another and raise our children. Ephesians 6:4 reads, "And ye fathers provoke not your children to wrath: but bring them up in the nurture and admonition of the Lord." KJV

Let's examine the word provoke. It means to anger, enrage, exasperate or vex. It means to stir up. It also means to arouse or call forth feelings, desires or activity. One of the dangers of provoking our children is that he or she may resent us for doing this. This type of behavior is damaging to the relationship and the child may carry this into adult life, if this emotional pain is not addressed.

The word nurture means to feed and protect, to support and encourage, to train, to educate. As parents we are privileged with a responsibility for the children given to us. God did not bless us to have children for us to order around, neglect or mistreat. Psalm 127:3-5 (Message) reads.

> 3 Don't you see that children are God's best gift? The fruit of the womb his generous legacy. 4 Like a warrior's fistful of arrows are the children of a vigorous youth. 5 Oh, how blessed are you parents, with your quivers full of children! Your enemies don't stand a chance against you; you'll sweep them right off your doorstep.

The final word in that verse that I want to visit is "admonition." It means to counsel, give advice or caution, a gentle reproof.

These verses of scripture are powerful. We must not only know these verses but implement them. In case you don't know, parenting is work. Sometimes we forget that our children have feelings. Although it seems that when they turn teens we feel like they are aliens from another planet. It's easy to yell at a child for doing something wrong. But it takes effort and love to gently correct them. Children don't always know that they have done something wrong. Many parents need to calm down and use a teachable tone. It helps to explain to a child how something should be done and why.

For instance, if you tell a child to go wash the dishes and you discover the child did not use dish liquid don't blame the child if the dishes are dirty. Did you have the child watch you do it the right way? Training a child is not just telling him do this or don't do that. You must instruct them. Remember we are shaping our children to be great in the earth. We are the first stage in their development.

We help them in building character. We teach them

how to relate to others. We teach them how to be kind, respectful and thoughtful. We teach them to be thankful and merciful, to be peaceful and serving to others. We teach them to learn to do good and most of all to love God with all their heart, soul and strength.

When children grow up Gods way, they become assets to our families, communities, states and the nations. They have a purpose in life a destiny to fulfill. So let's help them in their journey by building them up and instilling in them values that will guide them and protect them. Their destiny in life is not what you want them to be. I know I'm about to mess with some of you parents, but keep reading. It's wrong to insist or force your child to pursue your dream for them.

For instance, Julia may love to draw. When you ask her what she wants for her birthday, she asks for art supplies. When Christmas comes around she wants the same thing. Julia loves to draw and draws on almost anything. She enjoys watching art shows and so on. This may annoy you because you want her to be a nurse or teacher. So you discourage her by saying things to sway her in your direction of thinking.

Don't push your child to a career they have no interest in. Just because you didn't accomplish your career choice don't force it on the child. As I say in my church sometimes when the pastor is making a point, I will say," That'll preach.

Values Over Good Looks

*H*ow do you teach your daughter to value qualities over good looks in a man? This can be challenging in our society because so much emphasis is put on the outer appearance. Television, commercials and magazines portray images of young men and women with perfect bodies. These models have no blemishes and are the perfect size according to them. They're dressed in designer clothing and have beautiful hair. Models are portrayed with no scars and perfect noses. Their message says this is how we should look. These images are appealing to our youth. These images have power to influence them and they daydream about looking a certain way. Could there be a subliminal message that if or youth does not look like the images portrayed they are not cool or accepted?

As a result of this our youth make poor choices when it comes to the opposite sex.

These are only surface attractions that have no depth. The outside may be pleasing to the eyes, but inwardly this person may be shallow, obnoxious, rude, vindictive and selfish.

Not only that but our human nature through our eyes sees what looks good and desires what we see. Have you ever seen a beautiful lady with a man not so attractive? The first thing we say or think is," What does she see in him? Maybe you've seen a handsome man and a not so attractive lady with him. Is it possible there were qualities in those individuals that meant more to them for building a relationship than their good looks. Let's face it, looks aren't everything. I will admit it helps though; it just can't be the focus. We should teach our daughters not to be deceived by good looks.

Good looks don't matter when the bill collector calls. Good looks don't matter when the lights get turned off. Good looks don't matter when there's no money in the bank account or when the car gets repossessed. Who needs a good looking man if he spends his paycheck as soon as he gets it? When he neglects to take care of his family or is unfaithful. We must teach or daughters that there is much more to be desired than physical attractions.

Now let's get back to the question. It all starts with how the husband treats the wife. Of course the wife has a part to play as well. I'm focusing on the dad now because girls tend to select men like their dad. Some girls may not be aware that this is happening. Here are some of the qualities that make up a good man and should be displayed at home. Kindness, gentleness, respect, appreciation, compassion, sensitivity, caring, loving and let's not forget a good listener. I can go on but you get the picture. Fathers ask yourself," What kind of son in law do I want for my daughter?" Put the gun away and ask yourself. You should give that question serious thought. My prayer is that if you are not doing the right things you will begin now. Can your daughter say," I want to marry a man like my father who treats my mom with respect?"

When a young lady tells me she has met someone, one of the questions I ask her is," what's his relationship with his mother?" You might ask why that is important. I'm glad you asked. If a son is rude and disrespectful to his mother, chances are he will be rude to you, her mother and her.

As a father, you would not appreciate a young man telling your daughter to shut up in the middle of a conversation. Nor, would you like it if he made her feel inferior. Did you know that some men think that the only place for a woman is in the bedroom and the kitchen?

Some men feel women should be seen and not heard. This is a learned behavior. And in many cultures these attitudes toward women still exist. If your daughter is interested in someone of a different nationality it would be wise to study his customs and beliefs.

This is not the way to treat your wife. If the daughter believes this is normal behavior she will miss the obvious signs that she should avoid any young man who acts this way.

Communication

*R*achel and Bill have been married for five years. About a year ago they had their first child. Life as they once knew it has changed to say the least. Bill has been working longer hours to support his family. Rachel doesn't have as much free time any longer to help volunteer at the church. Some days seem to be longer than others and some nights aren't long enough. Rachel and Bill have not had much quality time with one another since the addition to the family.

Their anniversary is two weeks away. Rachel is excited and anticipating their weekend away. She has figured Bill will make dinner reservations and make reservations at the Hilton or some other fine hotel like he has done in the past.

Finally, the day has come. They've had breakfast

together and Bill is just about to leave. While kissing Bill on the lips she says, Honey, do you know what today is? He replies," Yes, its Friday and walks out the door.

Rachel has arranged for her in-laws to pick up Jr. around 4pm for the weekend. She then starts getting ready for their dinner and weekend out. Bill should be home around 5:30 pm. Instead Bill arrives around 7pm to find his wife in a beautiful evening dress and anxious to get the evening started. While greeting her he asks why are you dressed up? She responds," You didn't." He in turn replies," I didn't what." She says," You forgot our anniversary."

Do you know what happened next? That's right; she put him in the Dog House.

My husband and I have the pleasure of counseling married couples and we also teach a pre-marital class. We have discovered that communication is one of the top three reasons marriages end in divorce. The scenario above is a prime example of what can happen if there is a breakdown in communication. Rachel assumed that Bill would not forget their anniversary. When couples have conflict the tendency is to argue, call each other names or the silent treatment. Couples have not learned how to fight fair.

Daughters, Guns, and Bibles

Are you familiar with the term, dad is in the dog house? You may have even heard the man tell another man he was in the dog house. I dislike that statement and behavior. Your daughter should never wake up and find dad sleeping on the sofa or in another room. I do know that sometimes the wife chooses to sleep in another room. How does this look to our children? How does this type of behavior affect them? What message are we sending to our children? Our heat of the moment choices will cause pain for the entire family. Stop thinking that what you do doesn't affect anyone else. We are deceived if we think that way.

The Dog House treatment opens the door for Satan to destroy our family. The plot of Satan begins. You may find yourself in a vulnerable situation that leads to infidelity. I caution husbands and wives not to expose one another to friends, family and co-workers. In many cases this was done and the listener saw it as an opportunity to move in on your spouse. This is all because you planted a seed, "The Dog House Seed."

As husbands and wives we need to be mindful of the covenant we made to each other on our wedding day. We know that marriage is not always a bed of roses. There will be bumps in the road. After all, there are no perfect people and no perfect marriage. We will be faced with opportunities that will challenge our relationship. Marriage is work, a lot of work. Life happens to all of us. We must learn to communicate our differences like adults and not three year olds. Let's forgive and grow together. We are more powerful together than separate.

Actions Speak Louder Than Words

*I*t is said that to the degree we live our lives as Christians or non-Christian our seed will excel us. In other words, you may have one affair but your child may have two or more affairs. You may only smoke one pack of cigarettes a week and your child may smoke two or more a week. Or maybe it's alcohol. I'd like for that to happen in the spiritual sense. If I do one missionary trip, my child does two or more. If I lead 100 souls to Christ, my child will lead 200 or more. As time goes on progression takes place in the natural and spiritual realm.

We can lead by example. Have you heard the saying," actions speak louder than words? Our behavior speaks louder than the words we say. Many parents make the mistake of telling their children do as I say not as I do. Some children chose not to do the negative but others won't.

Some of us have learned the hard way. A person may look good on the outside but inwardly it's a different story. If you are age 40 or more you may have discovered that looks fade, the belly bulges, the chin doubles and some things are afraid of height. Are you thinking it's time to remove the clothes off the treadmill or elliptical right now?

Society can make you think that any couple that looks good together has a good marriage, wrong!!! Some started their relationship on a physical attraction and neither one got to know each other as a person. Things like values and beliefs? Is this person dependable, is he lazy or careless. Is he stable or confident? Is he trustworthy? Does this person have a job? Is this person just looking to have a good time or make a lifetime commitment? Some may have issues that you don't want to be a part of. These are some of the things to instill in your daughter. There are many more questions?

Dad, there is more to raising a daughter than just being a provider. Does your daughter hear and see you appreciate mom? I admire moms, especially those who are blessed to stay at home and pour into their children. What a beautiful thing that is. Let's hear it for the moms. There's not a salary that can compensate her for what she does. She does more than clean house, cook meals, have babies, change diapers or do the laundry. She's more valuable than the president of the United States of America. She is the CEO of her home; she's like the captain aboard a ship. She's an accountant, manager, teacher, developer, trainer and coach. She's a nurse and much more. She's the engine that keeps the house running. Husbands, don't be stingy with your applauds for her. As a matter of fact, you ought to pause right now and give her some praise. That's right, put this book down and give her praise. Go on, you can do it. I promise you won't regret it.

Husbands need to show appreciation to their wives on a regular basis. Don't wait for Mother's Day or Valentine's Day or her birthday. If you are guilty of doing that, raise your right hand and say these words. I will not wait for a holiday to appreciate my wife. Sit down and talk to your daughter. Tell her why you adore and appreciate her mother. This will also teach your daughter to value her mom and to show respect for her. Remember children will almost always emulate their parents. Little girls like to walk around in moms high heel shoes. They like to put on makeup like mom and carry a purse. Little boys like to play with tools like their dad. They try on dads neck ties and wear their shoes. Some even put on shaving cream and attempt to shave. If you walked into a class room of third or fourth graders and asked them who do they want to be like, you will probably get the same answer from every child. I want to be like my dad or I want to be like my mom. How sweet is that?

You should be there hero and role model. Not some athlete or television actor.

Love in Action

*L*oving your wife goes far beyond working on a job to keep a roof over the families head. It's more than making sure there are groceries in the house for mom to cook. Or making sure you have electricity or running water. Bringing home the paycheck does not replace telling your wife that you love her. I remember looking at some old black and white movies and seeing scenes where the woman asks the man," Do you love me?" And he replies, "You know I do." He would not say it. That may have been acceptable back then but not these days. I repeat bringing home the bacon is not enough. Women need to hear these words often. It's not enough to just say it in the bedroom either.

Does your daughter see First Corinthians the thirteenth chapter lived out in your home?

Just think if moms and dads lived by this the rate would not be as high as it is. People would i. married with the attitude of if it doesn't work I'll just get a divorce. Marriage is work. It's not the wife giving 50% and the husband giving 50%. Each one should give 100% to the marriage.

Daughters need to see dad hug on mom or kiss her on the cheek. She needs to hear her dad compliment or praise her mother. Does she see her father comfort mom in times of pain or encourage her when things are not working the way she has planned. Or does she hear dad putting mom down. What about helping mom with the dishes or laundry especially when mom is not well. Does she see the dishes pile up in the sink and laundry get backed up. What about vacuuming the carpet?

Your daughter needs to see love in action. Love, as God our heavenly father intended is not selfish. It puts others above us. It says the other person is more important. When a child sees this kind of love exhibited at home she is convinced that this is how a family should be. She will desire to have a husband that will treat her the way her dad treats her mother.

Of course when the child is old enough she can help with the chores. This is good for young men too, so that they learn to help their wives.

Husbands don't be afraid to love your wives openly. The rewards are worth it. Don't just tell her that you love her but show it also. You won't regret it. After all, you want her to be around for a long time.

Remember you have to do more than bring home the bacon. Think about this, let's say you have a motorcycle and you enjoy riding it every chance you get. Only you can describe the thrill of it. Well in order to ride you must take care of it. You must wash it, change the oil and even get a tune up. It may need new tires or brakes and of course gasoline.

Let's say you and your buddies have been planning a trip to Alaska on your bikes. You're all packed and ready to go. You go to your garage to start the bike and she doesn't sound right or maybe a tire is flat. Maybe she's out of gas. The point is if you want your baby to keep running efficiently you must take care of her. Of course I'm not comparing a wife to a motorcycle, but I think you get the picture.

Again husbands love your wives. When you love you won't abuse. When you love you won't neglect. I do realize that many men need to be taught how to treat a woman. They do all the right things during the courtship. After he has won the prize he seems to think he doesn't have to continue to do nice things. Hello!!!!

Unfortunately, many women have husbands that learned wrong behavior. He may have learned it from his father; step father or moms live in boyfriend. Or maybe there was no man in the house at all. Because of this we have a generation of men who mistreat women. I'm reminded of the scripture found in Hosea 4:6. The first part of that verse reads, "My people are ruined because they don't know what's right or true." (The Message Bible) I'm not trying to take this verse out of context but if you think about it, if you don't have knowledge about how something should work you will misuse or abuse it. A hammer is not designed to be used as a staple gun. A ladder was not designed to mow the lawn. If you don't know the purposes of something go to the manual. Some of these young men may have seen mom get slapped around or punched in the face or kicked. He may have called her dirty names. He may have been the kind of male figure who came home from work and all he does is watch television, eat then sleep. These days we find more and more men who play games on their computer or television. We even have cell phones with games on them. Many men are being distracted from their families. These things can and will rob families of the nurturing it needs to function properly.

If you don't know how to love your wife go to the bible. The Message version of Ephesians 5:25 says, Husbands, go all out in your love for your wives, exactly as Christ did for the church-a love marked by giving, not getting.

It does not say love your wives if she is kind to you, or love your wives if she doesn't burn the food. It doesn't say love your wives if she agrees with you. We must have unconditional love. This kind of love gives without reservation. There are no strings attached. The love Christ gave was given while we were yet sinners. Jesus saw the type of people we were and said I don't care how bad they are, they need a Savior and I will die for them. There is no greater love than that.

We use this word inappropriately. We say things like, I love that dress or I love those shoes. Our affection for dresses and shoes or even a football game is not the same as the love for another person. Let's examine the word love. There are three types:

Agape: The love of God or Christ for humankind. This is an unselfish love of one person for another without sexual implications. This love does not seek anything in return.

Eros: This type of love is self-centered. It is inspired by selfish human nature. This type of love has conditions attached to it.

Phileo: This type of love is a mutual attraction between two people; a brotherly love among friends.

The book of Ephesians instructs us on how to love. In the fifth chapter we are told to be imitators of God as dear children and walk in love. Husbands it's time to imitate the Father and be a follower of His. This goes for wives also. Let's take a look at verses 21 thru 33 from the Message Bible.

Out of respect for Christ, be courteously reverent to one another. Wives understand and support your husband's in ways that show your support for Christ. The husband provides leadership to his wife the way Christ does to his church, not by domineering but by cherishing. So just as the church submits to Christ as he exercises such leadership, wives should likewise submit to their husbands. Husbands go all out in your love for your wives, exactly as Christ did for the church-a love marked by giving, not getting. Christ's love makes the church whole. His words evoke her beauty. Everything he does and says is designed to bring the best out of her, dressing her in dazzling white silk, radiant with holiness. And that is how husbands ought to love their wives. They're really doing themselves a favor-since they're already one in marriage. No one abuses his own body, does he? No, he feeds and pampers it. That's how Christ treats us, the church, since we are part of his body. And this is why a man leaves father and mother and cherishes his wife. No longer two, they become one flesh. This is a huge mystery, and I don't pretend to understand it all. What is clear to me is the way Christ treats the church. And this provides a good picture of how each husband is to treat his wife, loving himself in loving her, and how each wife is to honor her husband.

Wow, that is powerful. I know that if we are faithful to follow these instructions we can experience heaven on earth. We have got to do it Gods way. Romans 15:4 (NKJV) reads, "For whatever things were written before were written for our learning, that we through patience and comfort of the Scriptures might have hope.

Lets look at the phrase," just as Christ also loved the church" in Ephesians 5:25. So how does Christ display His love for us the church? In Jeremiah 29:11 we find that God has good thoughts about us, thoughts of peace not evil, He has plans to give us a future and hope.

A husband can follow this example by being thoughtful of his wife, by thinking and planning ways to bless her. He can give her reasons to look forward to spending the rest of her life with him. He can prove faithful in the promises he makes to her so her hope will remain and she will trust him to take care of her. She needs security. This is one of the ways to fireproof your marriage.

In Zephaniah 3:17 the Lord rejoices over his children with singing. In other words He calms us with His love. A husband does this by complimenting and encouraging his wife. Not by amplifying her mistakes.

The 23 Psalm is a beautiful picture of the Lords love towards us. In verse one, He leads us, guides us and shields us. This is something that the husband should do as well. In verse two, He causes us to lie down in green pastures besides still and restful waters. Husbands will have peaceful wives when he takes care of his wife. He will in turn come home to a peaceful haven. In verse three, the Lord refreshes and restores us. A husband keeps the marriage fresh when he brings home flowers or leaves love notes or calls his wife during the day. In verse four, even when we walk through the valley of the shadow of death we will not be afraid because the Lord is with us and He comforts us with His rod and staff. As wives sometimes our days can be overwhelming. Things break in the house, the car doesn't start or maybe the children are being challenged to get along. Sometimes it's a Calgon take me away day. But, don't fear. Your hero will soon come home and make it all right. He'll fix what's broken. In verse five, the Lord prepares a table before us in the presence of our enemies and anoints our head with oil. Sometimes we may feel inadequate as a mother. Maybe you have a friend or neighbor who never burns a meal. Or you may have friends whose home is always spotless. Maybe you are struggling to lose that extra ten pounds. Because of this, Satan starts feeding you thoughts that steal your peace and cause you to put yourself down. A husband that loves his wife the way Christ loves us will not let you put yourself down or compare yourself with others.

He will confirm you and emphasize the great qualities and talents you possess. He will do this because you are unique and wonderfully made. Finally verse six tells us that goodness and mercy will follow us all the days of our life. Because our husbands will love like Christ loves, we can rest assured that our husband will be good to us and show us mercy when we are struggling. There's no husband like a Psalm 23 husband!

Unequally Yoked

✹

I remember when I was around 17 or 18 years old, I began attending an apostolic church. I heard this lady say that this couple we worked with was unequally yoked. I thought she was referring to them not being the same height. So I thought if I dated someone who was not my height I would be disobeying God. Fortunately, understanding came which was good, because I'm 4'10 and my husband is 5'10.

The term unequally yoked is found in 2 Corinthians 6:14-15.

2 Cor. 6:14 (Amp)
> Do not be unequally yoked with unbelievers [do not make mismated alliances with them or come under a different yoke with them, inconsistent with your faith].

> For what partnership have right living and right standing with God with iniquity and lawlessness? Or how can light have fellowship with darkness?

2 Cor. 6:15 (Amp)

> What harmony can there be between Christ and Belial [the devil]? Or what has a believer in common with an unbeliever?

Why would God tell his children don't be unequally yoked? It's only because He loves us and wants to protect us. Is it possible that our heavenly father knows best? Of course it is. It's a fathers responsibility to protect and direct his children, all those who have accepted Jesus as their Savior. Salvation isn't just for escaping hell or as some would say fire protection. It's much more than that. God's plan for our lives is to do us good and to give us a future according to Jeremiah 29:11-12. He wants to give us life abundantly according to John 10:10.

We must walk in obedience to the word of God.

Before accepting Christ, we were sinners living in darkness and were driven by our own fleshly desires according to Ephesians 2:1-3.

Now If Christ has changed your nature, why would you date someone whose nature has not been changed? God desires a holy union between a man and a woman. Your destination is heaven bound. For an unbeliever, hell will be his place for eternity.

Look at what Revelation 21:8 says.

Rev. 21:8 (NKJV)
> But the cowardly, unbelieving, abominable, murderers, sexually immoral, sorcerers, idolaters, and all liars shall have their part in the lake which burns with fire and brimstone, which is the second death."

If you have been born again of God, then why would you want to date or marry a person who is not? To do so is clearly an act of disobedience to the one who gave His life for you. This is not wise and you are asking for trouble. Many young girls and older women are deceived into thinking that she will change him and lead him to Christ while dating. No one can change a person but God. This is one of the oldest tricks of Satan. If you are a born again stop searching for a husband and search after God. You are not to find a husband, he finds you. Proverbs 18:22 reads,"Whoso findeth a wife findeth a good thing and obtains favor from the Lord." The man does the finding not the woman. It doesn't say whoso findeth a husband.

In many cases girls are anxious and disobey the word of God. They do not trust that God will give them a husband. They become impatient. And it gets even more difficult when it seems all their friends are marrying. The pressure gets to be too much for them and they don't know how to handle it. Anxiousness is an emotion that will lead you down the wrong path and cause you to make choices that can ruin your life. Many have not waited on God and are living to regret it. They have discovered that the man they were dating is not the man they married. They are abusive physically and verbally or men who abuse alcohol or drugs. Some have children or previous wives they failed to tell you about. Some have financial problems or a past that will haunt the marriage. Some are lazy and immature. He expects the wife to go out and work and he stay home and spend the money and hang out with the guys.

The book of Proverbs says that the righteous should choose their friends carefully, for the way of the wicked leads them astray. This is a trick of Satan to draw you away. You cannot be friends with the world and walk after God at the same time. You must choose. If you were a drug user before you accepted Christ and he delivered you and took away the desire for drugs, does it make sense to hang out with them?

If your former life consisted of cursing, smoking, drinking, sexual impurities and other works of the flesh, does it make sense to continue associating with people who practice that kind of lifestyle? Many of us had parents that told us don't hang out with the wrong crowd because they did not want us to be like that crowd. They did not want us to pick up bad habits. This passage of scripture is saying the same thing. Proverbs 22: 5 says," Thorns and snares are in the way of the perverse; he who guards his soul will be far from them." If you value your soul you will run from people who mean you no good. Don't be entangled with those who do not walk in the light. If you trust God's plan of salvation then trust him to give you the mate of His choice.

In the book of 1Kings the 11 chapter King Solomon had many foreign wives. He knew that he was not to marry these women because they would turn his heart to their gods. And so it was as he got older.

Let me tell you about a man who was born to deliver

the Israelites from the bondage of the Philistines. The Philistines were heathens, idol worshippers and they hated Gods people and ruled over them. His name was Samson. When his mother was pregnant with him an angel appeared to her and told her not to drink wine or beer and do not eat anything unclean. She was told not to cut his hair. When Samson was old enough to marry he saw a girl in Timnah that he liked a lot. She was a Philistine. He requested his parents get her for him to marry. His parents were not happy. He was taught not to be involved with the Philistines. They said, "Is there no woman among the daughters of your brethren, or among all my people, that you must go and get a wife from the uncircumcised Philistines?" In our words that would be, can't you find a godly woman of our faith to marry. They were saying, "Samson don't be unequally yoked to a heathen."

After Samson's marriage during the feast he was given 30 companions to whom he posed a riddle. If they could solve it he would give them 30 linen garments and 30 changes of clothing. If they could not solve it they would have to give him 30 linen garments and 30 changes of clothing. They had seven days to solve the riddle. His companions threatened to burn his wife and her relatives if she did not get the answer out of Samson. She enticed him for seven days until he gave in. She betrayed her husband for fear of the threat. Samson knew that these men had used his wife to get the answer.

Then the Spirit of the Lord came upon him and he killed 30 men of Ashkelon and took their clothing. He gave the clothing to his companions. After that Samson's wife was given to his best man. From then on Samson's anger grew and he sought vengeance. He set out to destroy the Philistines. Along the way he killed many.

Later he saw a harlot in Gaza and was intimate with her. There were men waiting to kill him. But he escaped taking with him the doors to the gate of the city and the posts. Sometime later he fell in love with a woman named Delilah. Are you beginning to see the type of women he choose to be with. It all started with one act of disobedience. He is now with a third woman.

The lords of the Philistines told Delilah to entice him to find out where his strength lies. They wanted to overtake him and afflict him. Each one of them offered her 1100 pieces of silver. Three times Samson told Delilah what would weaken him and she would say,

"Samson the Philistines are upon you." He would jump up and free himself from whatever she had bound him with. Finally she cried, "If you loved me you would not mock me. Samson should have gotten out of there like a gazelle. You can't dance with the devil and expect to come out a winner. Satan will whisper in your ear lies. He'll tell you, you can date that unbeliever and get him saved. God will forgive you. What Satan the deceiver won't tell you is shame comes with disobedience. Disobedience breeds disaster and heartache. It will bring you troubles. Delilah nagged him until he gave in. He told her no razor has ever come upon his head. He has been a Nazirite to God from his mother's womb and that his strength would leave him if his head is shaved. After he told the truth she lullabied him to sleep and called for a man to shave his hair. She then tormented him and saw that his strength was gone. She said, "Samson the Philistines are upon you. He awoke and shook himself like he did many times before, but this time the Spirit of the Lord had departed from him. The Philistines bound him, put his eyes out and made him a grinder in their prison.

There's an old saying that goes like this:

"Sin will take you farther than you want to go. Cost

you more than you want to pay and keep you longer than you want to stay.

Don't be pressured by family or coworkers who think you ought to be married by now. They say things like," you still single or what's wrong with you? How about this one? "You're not getting any younger." Statements like that can weigh on your emotions. Don't let it, shake it off. Some women are married and wish they were not. Their married and feel like their single. She may be married to him but he's not married to her. Your heavenly father wants to protect you from these types of situations. Let him. Proverbs says, "Hear, ye children, the instruction of a father, and attend to know understanding. For I give you good doctrine, forsake ye not my law. (Proverbs 4:1-2)

If you are involved with an unbeliever break it off now. God will honor your decision to obey Him and bless you with a husband that will love you as Christ loved the church. I am confident of this. One day I made that choice and I have never regretted it. I've been married for 31 years to the same man. There are moments when I wonder what I did to deserve such a wonderful husband. My husband found me, I did not find him.

Is He the Right One?

✻

Now I want to caution you. Just because this young man is a believer does not mean he's the one. You want a mature Christian man. I personally think a woman should desire a mate who is more mature in Christ than she is. You should want him to lead you closer to Christ and not you leading him. His walk with Christ should draw you closer to the Lord. Sometimes I tell my husband that I want to be like him when I grow up. You should desire someone that is sold out to God. You don't want to waste time on someone who is not sold out to God. Someone who comes to church when he feels like it is not serious about Christ. You don't want a man who is not self-controlled or lives by his emotions. You don't want a man who is self-centered. You don't want someone who thinks he is God's gift to women. Men like these are flight risks.

If you are being pursued by a man who claims he is a Christian and he drinks, smokes and likes to party, get rid of him. I seriously doubt that this person has made a real commitment to follow Christ.

A young lady should carefully seek God in prayer about any man that wants her attention. This is your life. Your emotions must not lead you. Ask God for signs so that your heart doesn't make the wrong choice. Seek counsel from mature women of God. Women who are submitted to their husbands the way God ordained. Make yourself accountable to someone who loves you enough to tell you when you are wrong. The bible says, "Where there is no counsel, the people fall; but in the multitude of counselors there is safety." (See Proverbs 11:14) God is concerned about our relationships and the covenants we make. His word tells us to acknowledge Him in all our ways and He will direct our paths. (See Proverbs 3:6)

Here is a list of questions you may want to ask yourself:

1. Is he born again?

2. Is he a member of a bible believing church?
3. Does he tithe?
4. Is he faithful in church attendance?
5. Is he serving in an area of ministry at church?
6. Is he submitted to authority?
7. Is he seeking the kingdom of God first?
8. Is he faithful in reading the word of God?
9. Does he have a prayer life?

The answers to these questions will help you to discern while you are waiting for the spouse you deserve. Notice I said," the spouse you deserve."

Because you are a child of God, you deserve the best man He has for you. He's not going to give you someone who will not appreciate you. The bible says He would not withhold any good thing from those who walk uprightly. (See Psalm 84:11)

The key to marrying the right person is found in your obedience to God. You must obey. Too many times girls have chosen to disobey being led by their flesh. They are so desperate that they connect to the first thing in a pair of pants. In their desire to marry quickly anyone who will pay attention to them, their heart overrides that still small voice on the inside. In the dating game, there are many signs along the way, but they get ignored. Don't ignore those signs. They may come from the voice of a youth leader, a counselor or co-worker. Perhaps your best friend sees things you don't see. I tell women they need someone who loves Jesus more than wanting to be with them. You want someone who loves Jesus more than anyone or anything else. Don't settle for anyone. You are special and unique. God has the right mate for you. Trust your heavenly father. Serve Him with all your heart and soul and mind.

Father Knows Best

✳

Many of us as a teenager thought our father was too strict and that he was old fashioned. We even thought he was dumb or didn't have a clue. He would not let us have our way when we wanted to hang out with some people or go places. We felt like everybody else is going or doing except me. Funny how every generation experiences that. Some of us later found out when we had children of our own that our parents were right in many ways. It wasn't that they didn't want us to have fun, they knew what could happen if they allowed us certain privileges. We would not remember that they were once our age.

The wisdom of a good father is priceless. To override his instruction can be detrimental to our wellbeing. We do not set out to disappoint our father we just want to do what we think is right in our own eyes.

In our relationship with Jesus we do not set out to disappoint him. Yet we do each time we disobey. As natural parents we feel the pain that comes when our children disregard our instructions. It is a painful feeling. We try to protect our children from mistakes. We say things like don't ride your bike in the street you may get hit by a car. Don't touch the stove it will burn you. Don't hang with the wrong crowd, associating with the wrong people will corrupt morals or cause you to be at the wrong place at the wrong time. We give them rules and boundaries. Is that because we are strict? Of course, it is not. A parent who does not give instructions to his child does not love his child.

Our heavenly father knows how to protect us. He has given the word of God to teach and guide us through life. Of course, the bible is not about dos and don'ts; it's about having an intimate relationship with Him. As we draw near to Him, we can experience His love for us. This may be difficult to do if you have not experienced the love of an earthly father. It may be hard to believe or accept the Heavenly Father's love. When you know without a shadow of a doubt that God loves you, you can trust the instructions He gives to you. When Satan comes around trying to tempt you to get involved with an unbeliever you can resist. You can walk away feeling good that you obeyed your heavenly father and have made Him proud of you.

In the natural every little girl wants to make her daddy proud. Young lady make Him proud. Make Him smile. You must know and be confident that God will send you a man worthy of you. If God was willing to sacrifice his only begotten son, how much more would he prepare and send you the man he has purposed for you. Wait on the Lord, wait for his blessing. He did say that he would not withhold any good thing from you. I know this is easier said than done. So while you are waiting find a place to serve in His kingdom.

Enjoy your relationship in Christ and grow where He has planted you. Focus on developing into the woman of God you were destined to be. After all, God always wants to give his little girl the Best!!!

Deception

✸

I once knew a lady years ago who was a Christian and a faithful church member. She had been divorced for a while. Well she met a man who was not a born again Christian. He began coming to church regularly and appeared to be interested in her way of life. Within months he proposed marriage to her. She was counseled to dissolve that relationship. She did not. After they married he stopped coming to church. He told her he did not want her coming to church. Do you know what happened next? She left the church.

That man deceived her. She opened the door to deception when she disobeyed Gods instruction: Do not be unequally yoked to unbelievers.

Another woman I knew years ago became involved with a man that broke her heart and the heart of her children from another relationship. After being counseled to not marry him she did. She discovered he was an alcoholic and the marriage ended in divorce.

I know of relationships where the husband does not let his wife come to church. Some men will not allow their wives to give tithes or offerings. Some men are jealous of the Pastor. These things can be avoided if obedience is followed.

Satan has deceived women into thinking that she can change him. No one can change another person. Satan causes her to think that she can't afford to let this one get by. Or she thinks she's got to have a man and any man will do. If you think that way you are selling yourself short. Set yourself free from that kind of mentality. You are the princess in God's kingdom and He has a prince for you.

I am not saying that when you marry a godly man that you won't have challenges in your marriage. We live in a world of temptations and distractions. I am saying a marriage has a better chance of success when founded in obedience. The need to obey the word of God far outweighs your desire to be married.

There will be times when Satan will attempt to bring division in your marriage. Then there are times when we allow ourselves to be agitated with one another. The fact that two people who think differently living under one roof can be a learning experience. Many times opposites attract. He may not squeeze the tube of toothpaste to your liking. The fact that he doesn't put the toilet seat down may irritate you. Especially if you have sat down before noticing the seat was up. He may be messy and you are a neat freak. Maybe he puts the toilet tissue on the roll backwards or leaves his towel on the floor after showering. Of course these are minor things and should not cause tension in the relationship. You would be surprised to learn how many couples have sat in a counselor's office about things like this. He may have an anger issue when things don't go his way. Maybe he's the jealous type or possessive. These are just a few things you may not discover while courting. We all grew up in different home environments. Not every family grew up having dinner around the table sharing their day as they ate. His family probably ate in front of the television. Maybe he was not raised to share his feelings or told men don't cry. He may want to practice a family tradition that you strongly dislike. He may only go to church on Easter or Christmas. He may not celebrate the same holidays as you. You may differ on how to raise children. He may not want children and you do. He may want two children and you want five. You may differ in your religion. Are you getting the picture I'm painting?

If you are not discerning, you will be deceived. Anyone can talk Christian lingo. But a deceiver cannot bear fruit. Beware of the charmer. Charm is deceptive. Charm will mess with your emotions and fleshly desires. Charm can be used to manipulate you into doing something you would not do on your own. Those sweet lines will make your head swim. Here are some of those lines he speaks with a smile of deception.

a. Girl, you are too pretty to be single.
b. Girl, you are too intelligent for that Christianity stuff.
c. You don't really believe in that stuff?
d. I can't believe someone hasn't already married you.
e. I need a girl like you.
f. I can't live without you, girl.
g. You rock my world.
h. I've never met anyone like you.
i. I've been dreaming of a girl like you.

Run from the charmer. Run like the gazelle!!!

Many unsaved young and old men want a good Christian girl. He figures she won't cheat on him. She won't go out drinking and carrying on. She won't lie to him. He likes the thought of her being a virgin. Her purity attracts him to her because she is innocent. He's probably been around with different girls and now that he wants to settle down, he goes to church to find and conquer. He's not interested in serving God. Beware young lady. There are wolves in the church. Have you heard the saying, "the devil comes to church too?" I'm not calling him the devil but he is being influenced by Satan to snare you.

Don't be deceived when he walks in dressing the part. A package can look good until you accept it. You might discover a snake on the inside.

Be sober; be vigilant; because your adversary the devil walks about like a roaring lion, seeking whom he may devour. 1Peter 5:8 NKJV

So Your Daughter Wants To Date

Do you remember the day your daughter said I want a boyfriend? What happened to the time when she was content playing with her baby dolls or throwing the ball around with dad? What happened to the days when she did not like boys and beat them up? These are probably some of the thoughts going through your mind right now.

Let's face it. It was bound to happen sooner or later, preferably much later. Now she wants to wear lipstick and eye shadow. Maybe it's our fault that she is now interested in the opposite sex. Maybe you lived next door to a family who had a handsome little five year old boy and when he and your adorable five year old daughter played together you commented how cute

Daughters, Guns, and Bibles

they looked together. They may have been in the same class and went to the same birthday parties. Some parents start planning the future for the two of them to marry each other. We don't realize at the time that the teenage years are around the corner and their hormones will change them into another person. If you have a teenager you know what I mean.

Parents it's not our fault. It all started with Adam and Eve in the book of Genesis. It's natural for men and women to be attracted to one another.

Now back to this boyfriend thing. Some parents have restrictions. Some feel their daughter can't date till she is 16 or 18. Some feel not till she's 20. Another restriction is no dating on a weeknight. Or, maybe an adult has to be present. How about be home by 10 pm. Do any of these sound familiar.

When she announces she wants a boyfriend, does the dad pull out his gun to give it a good cleaning? Do you know what happens to a girl when she starts liking a boy? She may become emotional. Some girls get a little silly. Some become distracted or lose interest in hobbies. Some disconnect from the family. And if you attack the young man they become defensive.

In an interview with Linda and Dave about their

daughter, they shared a moment about Sarah's rebellious days. Dave went on to say that they always made their house available to her friends knowing that they were stoners. He didn't trust them but he would allow them to come over to the house. He said, "She always brought home these little skinny guys who weren't much bigger than a pen. One day upon returning home from work was a boy sitting on his front porch stoned. Dave stuck out his hand to greet him. (The boy cowered a bit) Dave would squeeze his hand. Dave smiling big would say," good to have you here.

Dave said I didn't dislike the boy I just knew he was the wrong person for my daughter. There were other friends that came around and Sarah would say to her father, "Dad you have to stop scaring my friend."

Dave's response was I didn't do anything-I just greeted them and Sarah replied," but your arms are so big." Since then her friends called him Popeye. To her friends those Popeye arms must have seemed like guns. His department was to instill fear in young men. They needed to know that she was his little girl no matter her age. I asked them what things they did to make her feel special. One of the things Linda would do is be on the couch when she came home from school in case she needed to talk. This was called the Couch Ministry. It's a family tradition even though Sarah is an adult now. Dave was blessed to work at a Bible Camp so on Saturdays the family got to swim and ski at the lake for free. Sometimes Sarah would use this time to talk to her dad.

They have taught Sarah to desire a man after Gods heart. And they have lived as examples of a good husband and mother. They have not gone to bed angry. The word of God has been there benchmark. They counsel themselves and their daughter in the word. Dave shared that when it comes to our daughters, dads need to walk out what it means to be strong in faith, strong in conviction, to work hard and to love our wives. Linda shared that some of the things her daughter saw in their relationship is that her dad really loved her mom. She likes how they openly express their love to one another and that they are playful. This is something Sarah desires to have in her marriage. Dave shared that he would not be the man of God he is if Linda was not the woman of God she is. That is powerful. If that wasn't good enough he said. "Linda would not be the woman of God she is, if he wasn't the man of God he is. That speaks volumes.

Hope

✳

*H*ow do you keep hoping when it seems you've waited so long? What do you do when hope dies? To do so is work. Its work to keep hope alive, especially when there is pain associated with it. In this chapter I want to share with you some tools to help in this journey.

As a father you can be instrumental in encouraging your daughter to not give up hope on one day marrying. She will need affirmation that she is worthy of a prince and that he is out there. The bond between a father and his daughter is strengthened when the two of them pray in faith for the man God has for her.

The remainder of this chapter, I want to address to daughters.

Sometimes when we get a promise from God to

give us a husband we try to help God out. We put up our antennas and every man we see we say "Is he the one?" We put our feelers out there. It's as if we forget that God who created heaven and earth all by Himself does not need our assistance. The placement of the stars and the moon was set in place before there was a woman. He divided the heavens and the earth without the help of anyone. Now since He did all of that alone, surely He can and will prepare and provide a husband for you. After all he does know you inside and out. He knew you before your parents got together. He knew you while you were in your mother's womb. It's important that we are intimately acquainted with God. If God prepared a plan of salvation thru His son Jesus, surely He can bring you a husband.

You might feel it is an impossible act. Maybe your past life without Christ speaks louder than your faith at times. I assure you, your past is the past. 2 Corinthians 5:17 tell us if anyone be in Christ he is a new creation, old things have passed away; behold all things have become new. Now that you are in Christ you are no longer the same person. A new life has begun and all your sins are forgiven. You are now identified with Christ. You have no past. The slate is clean. A new book is being written.

It's as if your life is a blank canvas and ready for God to paint a beautiful portrait. So let hope arise in you. Let hope be the brush that paints your future.

Hope by definition means the feeling that what is wanted can be had. When there is no hope, life can seem pointless. There's nothing to look forward to. That's why it is important to dream and dream big. Another word for hope is desire. What do you desire? Does it line up with God's word? If it does, then don't stop desiring. Proverbs 13:12 reads," Hope deferred makes the heart sick, But when the desire comes, it is a tree of life."(NKJV)

It is Gods will for you to desire. Here are a few scriptures. Psalm 37:4 reads, "Delight yourself also in the Lord, and He shall give you the desires of your heart.

We do this by spending time in his presence giving praise and worship to Him. When we adore him and proclaim His lordship in our lives. We don't just do this in church. We should do this in our home as well. Delighting in the Lord should be a lifestyle. As we delight in Him our desires become one with His will for us. We also do this by serving him and others in ministry whether in the confines of the local church or marketplace ministry. We should delight to do His will, that which brings glory to His name.

Isaiah 58:14 reads, "Then you shall delight yourself in the Lord; and I will cause you to ride on the high hills of the earth, and feed you with the heritage of Jacob your father. The mouth of the Lord has spoken."

There was a married woman who was barren. Yearly her husband would go to Shiloh to worship and sacrifice to the Lord. This was a very sad time for her. Even though her husband would give her a double portion for offerings it did not make her feel any better. You see her husband had a second wife name Pennant who had sons and daughters. Whenever they went to Shiloh this woman would provoke her and make her miserable because she was barren. Hannah the barren wife would be grieved in her heart and not eat.

On one of their trips Hannah went into the tabernacle and poured her heart out to the Lord. She asked the Lord to look on her affliction and remember her. If He would give her a male child she would give him to the Lord all the days of his life, and no razor would touch his head.

The priest Eli accused Hannah of being drunk because he saw her lips moving but heard no sound from her. She quickly explained that she was not a wicked woman; she was pouring her grief on the Lord. Eli then said to her, "Go in peace and the God of Israel grant your petition. She went her way and was no longer sad. The next morning Hannah and her family worshiped before the Lord and returned home. The bible says Elhanan knew Hannah, the Lord remembered her and she conceived and bore a son. His name was Samuel.

Hope has a way of changing your countenance. It will change the way you walk and talk. It brings a confidence that you will get what you have been hoping for. Hope will strengthen you and cause faith to work again.

Let me tell you about a Shunammite woman who declared, "It is well" while her son lie dead. There was a prophet by the name of Elisha and his servant Gehazi who traveled to Shunen. This woman perceived that Elisha was a holy man of God and convinced her husband to make a room for him so when he would come to town he could stay there. And her husband did. One day when he came to visit, he asked his servant Gehazi to call the woman and say to her, "you have cared for us, what can we do for you? Do you want me to speak to the king or the commander of the army on your behalf?" She said I dwell among my own people.

When she left their presence he said, "What can be done for her." Gehazi mentioned she has no son and her husband is old. Elisha had Gehazi call her back and told her," this time next year you shall embrace a son." She replied," do not lie to me man of God."

Well the man of God did not lie. She conceived and had a son. Some years went by and the child became ill and died. She laid the boy on the bed of the prophet. This woman sent to her husband for a rider and a horse. 1 can imagine this woman riding and saying, "It is well." The prophet returned with the Shunammite woman to her home and raised the child from the dead. This story is found in 2kings the fourth chapter.

God is the same yesterday, today and forever. What he's done for one he will do for others. He is not a respecter of persons. He's looking for faith filled people who will call those things which be not as though they were. So say what you are believing for. Many times our answers are delayed because we speak faith when we are among the believers but then when we are alone we speak doubt and unbelief. Whatever we say in public we need to say in private. So take courage and expect your desires to be fulfilled.

Questions and Answers

✽

*B*elow are some questions I asked some dear friends to answer.

Q. Was there ever a boy that your daughters brought home and you wished you had a gun?
A. Mom said there was this young man who put his hand on my daughters' thigh. A surprising instant anger rose in me and I thought if I had a gun I would hit him with it. Inwardly saying, "Don't touch my daughter." Dad's feelings were the same as hers.
Q. What type of things did you do with your daughters to make them feel special?
A. Dad said he would have daddy dates with his daughters and sons. On Thursday or Friday

he would go have lunch with them. A different child each week at their school or pick them up and take them to lunch and chat. For the girls he would open the car door. Mom shared that her husband showed a lot of affection to the children so they would not crave attention from somewhere else. From the time they were babies they would lay a blanket on the floor and give the babies massages and foot rubs. This continued, as they grew older with appropriate affection such as stroking the hair and shoulder massages when the children were tight while watching television or just talking together. Dad said he has no regrets and the girls have said the same. The girls said they are thankful they can tell their friends how they were cared for. They read the bible to them and had devotions with them. They also prayed a lot with them. They were given lots of scripture and were well versed. The girls knew that their parents did not believe in dating and they didn't desire to date. The daughter who is married had her first kiss the day of her proposal of marriage.

Q. What qualities have you taught your daughters

to look for in a young man as a possible mate?

A. The main thing is he needs to be a worshiper. He needs to be kingdom minded and hears from the Lord.

Q. When your daughters observe how you treat your wife, do they desire to have a husband that will treat her the same way?

A. Yes. They saw their dad treat me with respect. He helped me a lot around the house even changing diapers.

Dad shared that they would not have done the things they did with their children if it had not been for the resources that were made available to them by the church. They took classes and read books, and were surrounded by people who were doing it right. Dad said he didn't grow up with that kind of teaching and would not have done it with his own. They prayed a lot about how to discipline the children. Depending on the child's personality they would use a word, a look or a spanking. They didn't always do it right but the children knew they were earnestly seeking the Lord on how to do it. If they made a mistake they would apologize to them.